MW00653650

AFRICAN NAMES AND THEIR MEANINGS

AFRICAN NAMES AND THEIR MEANINGS

DR. S. OPUNABO ABELL

LeMoyne-Owen College,
Memphis

VANTAGE PRESS
New York

FIRST EDITION

Published by Vantage Press, Inc.
516 West 34th Street, New York, New York 10001

Manufactured in the United States of America
ISBN: 0-533-09675-8

0 9 8 7 6 5 4 3 2 1

To those most dear to me: my mother, Naneh, my children, Somieye, Olee, and Nene, and people of African descent who lost their original surnames.

Contents

Acknowledgments

I would like to thank all individuals who contributed to the completion of this book directly or indirectly. While space will not permit me to mention everybody individually, I am particularly grateful to Dr. Augustine Elosiebo, Dr. Meade Walker, Ms. Gretchen Walsh, Ms. Patricia Wilkins, Mr. Charles Radford, Ms. Linda McWilliams, Ms. Florence Obiako, Ms. Spanny Boyle, Mrs. Annie Hayes, and many others for their valuable assistance.

Preface

The motivation to compile this compendium of African names was provided by a friend and colleague, the late Dr. Waller of the African Studies Center at LeMoyne-Owen College. Dr. Waller spent five years in Africa on sabbatical, during which time he became thoroughly acquainted with the cultural symbolism of names on the African continent. There is a strong belief in African culture that children are influenced by the meanings of their names. For this reason, parents usually choose names with positive meanings for their children in the hope that these names will influence the children's personalities and inspire them to achieve. It is my hope that the names contained in this collection will serve the same cultural and developmental functions here as they do in Africa.

While this book does not claim to be the authority on African culture and history, it is one of the first books of its kind to compile a list of African names, in one book, from different countries. In compiling this book I was greatly aided by my many years of experience and understanding of African and American culture, having lived within both cultures for equal lengths of my life. To facilitate the use of this book by people whose native language is not African, extreme care was taken to select only those names that pose little phonetic and translational difficulties.

This book is arranged in sections, which makes its use and comprehension easy. The first section contains a summary of the history of the people of Africa. The second section, which is the main body of the book, lists the most popular African names, their meanings, and their origins. The third section, the appendices, contains illustrations that show the geographical areas covered by the major African language groups, and the early African kingdoms and empires. At the end of the book there is detailed bibliography for those who want to pursue topics on African and African-American literature.

"Afrocentricity": Its Significance*

When a lot of people, especially white people, hear the word *Afrocentricity,* they feel threatened, nervous or both. They shouldn't, [because, in the United States, as elsewhere] there have always been institutions that reflect and relate to particular constituencies. Brandeis and Yeshiva (for example) place a strong emphasis on the culture and experience of the Jewish people. Notre Dame and Georgetown acknowledge their Catholic roots. Vassar and Barnard have long been devoted to the empowerment of women. West Point and the Naval Academy obviously have strong ties to the nation's military establishment. Each of these institutions has its distinctive flavor, reflecting its constituency, and this flavor infuses its teaching and learning. Students of these institutions receive a solid grounding in whatever academic disciplines they choose to study alongside that special something.

No one accuses these institutions of advocating or practising cultural separatism or being propaganda mills. But whenever advocates of Afrocentricity speak of infusing a curriculum with an orientation that reflects the heritage of the people of African descent, all too often that is just what happens. Those making this accusation themselves could face

* The above is an excerpt from an article published in the *Washington Post* by Dr. Franklyn Jenifer, President of Howard University, Washington, D.C.

an accusation: of ignorance, ignorance of the rich tradition of special-interest institutions in this nation.

(Afrocentricity is often misunderstood by those who do not really care to find out its true meaning.) To regard Afrocentricity simply as a means to help African American youth to feel "good about themselves" is to take the narrow view. The key measure of Afrocentricity's validity is that it makes educational sense. An education that views the European heritage as central, and, by assumption, superior, and that views non-European heritages as peripheral, and, by assumption, inferior, is a deficient education. For it fails to prepare our youth for the reality of a world that is increasingly interdependent and a nation that will increasingly be composed of nonwhite peoples.

Afrocentricity isn't about exclusion. Afrocentricity is about inclusion, and that is something all people can understand.

AFRICAN NAMES AND THEIR MEANINGS

The People of Africa

Introduction

The continent of Africa covers a total land area equal the size of the United States and the Soviet Union combined. It has a population of about 650 million which is expected to rise to about 700 million by the year 2000. Demographically the population is about 80 percent black, 19 percent Arab and Berber, and 1 percent people of Asian and European descent. Africa is therefore predominantly populated by people of negroid descent.

A majority of the population lives in the rural countryside, but an increasing number of people are moving to cities in search of better paying jobs. This trend has dramatically increased the population in large cities, causing social and infrastructural problems typically associated with American and European cities. Some of the highly urbanized cities with populations greater than one million include Lagos, Port Harcourt, Ibadan, and Kaduna in Nigeria; Alexandria and Cairo in Egypt; Johannesburg and Capetown in South Africa; Algiers in Algeria; Abidjan in Ivory Coast; Casablanca in Morocco; Addis Ababa in Ethiopia; and Kinshasa in Zaire.

Africans speak many different languages. The most widely spoken languages are Swahili, Hausa, Yoruba, Ibo, Zulu, Xhosa, Malinke, Amharic, Berber, Arab, Fulani, Galla, Fante, Sotho, Ijaw, and Somali (see appendices A, B, and C).

Three main religions are practiced in Africa, namely:

Christianity, Islam and traditional African religion, also called animism. The term *animism*, as used here, refers to the worship of God through inanimate intermediary gods. Animists believe that God is too great and complex to be worshipped directly by man. Of the three religions, Christianity is the most widespread.

In terms of natural resources, Africa is the richest of all the continents. It has the world's largest reserve of gold, diamond, copper, nickel, platinum, manganese, cobalt, radium, bauxite, germanium, titanium, phosphate, and lithium. Other minerals present in very large quantities include iron ore, tin, zinc, chromium, thorium, lead, limestone, gypsum, zirconium, graphite, antimony, beryllium, vanadium, mica, sulphur, and natron.

Early History

Early historical records indicate that the first recorded permanent human settlement anywhere in the world developed in Africa along the Upper and Lower Nile Valley at about 5000 B.C. By 3100 B.C. the two Nile settlements were united under a single ruler to form ancient Egypt, which subsequently developed into an important learning center, serving among others, the early Greek, Roman, and Hebrew philosophers. Recent excavations in East Africa by the famous anthropologist, Richard Leakey, have further confirmed that Africa was the epicenter of human evolution and, by inference, the cradle of world civilization.

Between 1000 B.C. and the third century A.D., other settlements independently developed south of ancient Egypt and flourished as important commercial and learning centers. These included Sudan, Kush, Alodia, Mukurra, Nobatia, and Aksum which later became Ethiopia (see appendix D).

At about the fourth century A.D., the Romans conquered all the North African states, including Carthage, and absorbed them into the Roman Empire. The Romans used their newly acquired African kingdoms as granaries to support their empire. It could therefore be argued that the sustenance provided by the vassal African granaries enabled the Roman Empire to expand and last as long as it did. Also, subsequent evolution of Greco-Roman ideas and Western culture was, to a large extent, made possible by the lifeline provided by the early African kingdoms, especially Carthage and ancient Egypt. It was at about this period that Christ and His parents took refuge in ancient Egypt to escape the wrath of King Herod (see Matthew 2:13–23). Many historians therefore believe that Christ and his parents must have been black to have preferred refuge in a kingdom populated by black people. Along this line of reasoning, one can also say that Christianity would not have evolved if it were not for the safe haven provided by black ancient Egypt.

At about A.D. 640, after the death of Islamic Prophet Muhammad, Egypt and the other North African states were attacked and occupied by Arab jihadists who drove most of the original black inhabitants into the interior of the continent. It was for this reason that the present-day North African states, including Egypt, are predominantly Arabic today.

Era of Colonialism

Records and diaries of early European explorers indicate that before the first Europeans "visited" Africa in the fourteenth century, Africa had many prosperous and powerful empires, kingdoms, and city-states and many of these empires engaged in lucrative commercial activities with one another and became very prosperous in the process. Ancient Egypt, Sudan, and Kush, for example, were engaged in complex metal-smelting activities considered by many historians and anthropologists to be superior to, or in the least, comparable to those in contemporary Europe. Ironically, it was the prosperity resulting from this lucrative commerce that attracted European and Arab traders to invade and occupy the African kingdoms. So the point could be made that slave trade was not the initial interest of European explorers and traders in Africa. Slave trade became a major interest only after the Americas, the so-called new world, named after Amerigo Vespucci of Spain, were discovered.

The era of European colonialism and exploitation of Africa lasted for about four hundred years. During this period all normal human activities ground to a halt. Family life and other productive activities were disrupted as Europeans subjected Africa and Africans to centuries of chaos, deprivation, and slavery. Between the fourteenth and the eighteenth centuries A.D., entire cities and kingdoms of once free and proud kings, queens, princes, princesses, and their followers were enslaved and forcibly relocated to faraway places like the United States, Brazil, Jamaica, Bahamas, and Cuba. It must be remembered that for every one African that was successfully "repatriated" to these places, between five to ten other Africans either fought to the death or committed suicide.

The final digestion of Africa by the European powers occurred during the Berlin Conference of 1884 to 1885. In that conference, France, Britain, Germany, and Italy divided Africa among themselves into spheres of influence, establishing the present national boundaries of the African countries (see appendix E). And even though no African was present at the conference and none was signatory to the treaty, the African kingdoms were forced to observe the terms of the treaty. Thereafter, the continent of Africa was exploited to the bone while its human and material resources were used to develop

Europe and America. Today the same people that enslaved, pauperized, and undeveloped Africa are also the quickest to highlight Africa's comparative underdevelopment. It should again be remembered that, unlike the Jews who received hefty reparations and rehabilitation for six years of suffering during the Second World War, Africa and Africans were offered no help after four hundred years of deprivation and slavery. What Africa received instead was a new form of colonialism, also called neocolonialism. This is the practice of granting political independence while at the same time denying economic independence. The European colonial powers used this strategy to effectively undermine the political independence of the newly independent African states.

It is almost impossible to accurately convey the destructive impact that the slave trade and its aftermath had on the African continent. One can only say that it effectively set Africa's progress back by more than five hundred years. It is however amazing that despite these incredible odds, Africans and people of African descent all over the world still make significant contributions to world civilization. This is a laudable achievement and should be a source of pride. This pride should be underlined by an Afrocentric awareness and remind us that all people of African descent have a common cultural and genealogical heritage in Africa. Marcus Garvey aptly said it many decades ago:

"A people without the knowledge of their past history, origin and culture is like a tree without roots."

Names, Meanings, and Origins

Names	Meanings	Origin
Aali	Excellent	Kenya/ Tanzania
Abasi	God	Nigeria
Abayomi	God saves me	Nigeria
Abebe	Righteous man	Ethiopia
Abiola	Born into wealth	Nigeria
Abiye	My wish	Nigeria
Abu	Leader	Sierra Leone
Adabu	The polite one	Kenya/ Tanzania
Adedeji	Second to the king	Nigeria
Adeife	The king/crown is loved	Nigeria
Adeniyi	This is the king/crown	Nigeria
Adeyemi	Fit to be king	Nigeria
Adeyemo	This child will be king	Nigeria
Adhama	Dignity	Kenya/ Tanzania
Adhimisha	Praise, honor	Kenya/ Tanzania
Adili	Pure	Kenya/ Tanzania
Adinasi	Freeman	Kenya/ Tanzania
Adokiye	My ultimate desire/wish	Nigeria
Afua	Forgiveness	Kenya/ Tanzania
Agala	Love	Uganda
Ahadi	Promise, vow	Kenya/ Tanzania
Ahidi	Promise, vow	Kenya/ Tanzania
Aida	Princess	Ethiopia
Ainka	The cherished one	Nigeria

Names	Meanings	Origin
Ajali	Destiny, faith	Kenya/ Tanzania
Ajayi	We shall fight	Nigeria
Ajoke	Loved by all	Nigeria
Akanbi	First born	Nigeria
Akande	Second born	Nigeria
Akida	Leader	Kenya/ Tanzania
Akili	Competent, capable	Kenya/ Tanzania
Akin	Blessing	Nigeria
Akiniyi	A blessing	Nigeria
Akonte	I made it	Nigeria
Alabi	Born into wealth	Nigeria
Alabo	King	Nigeria
Alaye	Kingly, like a king	Nigeria
Almasi	Precious jewel	Kenya/ Tanzania
Amal	Hope	Egypt
Amana	Promise, vow	Kenya/ Tanzania
Amandah	Freedom	Sierra Leone
Amani	Peace and security	Kenya/ Tanzania
Amechi	Nobody can predict the future	Nigeria
Amina	Peaceful person	Kenya/ Tanzania
Amini	Faith, belief/Leader	Kenya/ Tanzania
Aminifu	Faithful, loyal	Kenya/ Tanzania
Aminika	Trustworthy	Kenya/ Tanzania
Anana	Gentle, tender	Kenya/ Tanzania
Anasa	Pleasant, pleasing	Kenya/ Tanzania
Anisi	Pleasing, delightful	Kenya/ Tanzania
Anozie	Looking good/well	Nigeria
Ariyo	We rejoice at what we see	Nigeria
Ashiki	Love, passion	Kenya/ Tanzania
Asikiya	I am not choosy	Nigeria

Names	Meanings	Origin
Asilia	Genuine	Kenya/ Tanzania
Asinobi	From the heart, heart-felt	Nigeria
Askari	Warrior	Kenya/ Tanzania
Atekeye	What I prayed for	Nigeria
Atinu	Pleasant, desirable	Nigeria
Ayinla	Praise the king/crown	Nigeria
Ayo	Happiness	Nigeria
Azana	Ultimate	South Africa
Azizi	Excellent	Kenya/ Tanzania
Azubike	The past is our strength	Nigeria
Azuka	Our past glory	Nigeria
Bahati	Good fortune, good luck	Kenya/ Tanzania
Bambisa	Pledge, vow	Zimbabwe
Bamidele	Come home with me	Nigeria
Baraka	Blessing, prosperity	Kenya/ Tanzania
Bariki	Blessed	Kenya/ Tanzania
Bayo	Rejoice with me	Nigeria
Belema	Love	Nigeria
Bibi	Miss, lady	Kenya/ Tanzania
Bidii	Intelligent	Kenya/ Tanzania
Bikira	Virgin	Kenya/ Tanzania
Bingwa	Competent, capable	Kenya/ Tanzania
Binti	Girl, daughter	Kenya/ Tanzania
Bismillahi	In the name of God	Kenya/ Tanzania
Boma	Blessing	Nigeria
Bongela	Compliment, praise	South Africa
Bora	Excellent	Kenya/ Tanzania
Bulungi	Goodness, good qualities	Uganda
Buraha	Comfort	Kenya/ Tanzania
Busara	Tactful, common sense	Kenya/ Tanzania
Chagina	Courage	Kenya/ Tanzania
Chasiri	Courage	Kenya/ Tanzania

Names	Meanings	Origin
Cheko	Good mood, happiness	Kenya/ Tanzania
Cheta	Always remember	Nigeria
Chetachi	Always remember God	Nigeria
Chibueze	God is the king	Nigeria
Chibuike	God is power	Nigeria
Chibuzor	God is the way	Nigeria
Chidi	God is alive	Nigeria
Chidozie	God is in charge	Nigeria
Chiedu	God is the leader	Nigeria
Chieke	God is the creator	Nigeria
Chigozi	God blesses	Nigeria
Chika	God is great	Nigeria
Chike	Power of God	Nigeria
Chikelu	God created all	Nigeria
Chikezie	God is the creator	Nigeria
Chima	God has the answer	Nigeria
Chimakara	God knows best	Nigeria
Chimara	God knows everything	Nigeria
Chimdi	My God is alive	Nigeria
Chimeka	Thanks to God	Nigeria
Chimela	Thanks to God	Nigeria
Chinasa	God cleanses	Nigeria
Chinedu	God leads, God guides	Nigeria
Chinyere	Gift from God	Nigeria
Chitara	The will of God	Nigeria
Chitunda	Dignity	South Africa
Chukudi	God is alive	Nigeria
Chukuka	God is the greatest	Nigeria
Chukuma	God has the answer	Nigeria
Chukumere	The will of God	Nigeria
Chuma	Famous, prominent; polite	South Africa

Names	Meanings	Origin
Dabiku	Sacrifice, offering	Kenya/ Tanzania
Dafina	Valuable, precious	Kenya/ Tanzania
Dagogo	Like father, junior	Nigeria
Daktari	Doctor, healer	Kenya/ Tanzania
Damisi	Sociable, cheerful	Kenya/ Tanzania
Damiso	Blessed one	South Africa
Dauda	Strong	Sierra Leone
Dibia	Wise man, healer	Nigeria
Dike	Tough guy, strongman	Nigeria
Dini	Faith, religion	Kenya/ Tanzania
Dorutimi	Stand by me	Nigeria
Dumisha	Intimate friendship	Kenya/ Tanzania
Ebele	Mercy	Nigeria
Eberechi	Grace of God	Nigeria
Ebi	Goodness	Nigeria
Ebidou	Search for that which is good	Nigeria
Echeruo	Deep thought, reflection	Nigeria
Eidi	Festival, festivity	Kenya/Tanzani
Ejike	We have the power	Nigeria
Ekang	He will overcome	Nigeria
Ekevu	Intelligent, enlightened	Kenya/ Tanzania
Ekong	Warrior	Nigeria
Elechi	Hope in God	Nigeria
Elewa	Very intelligent	Kenya/ Tanzania
Elimu	Knowledge	Kenya/ Tanzania
Emeka	Great deed	Nigeria
Emenike	Force solves no problem	Nigeria
Eneme	Cheerful	South Africa
Eno	Gift	Nigeria
Enyi	Precious friend	Nigeria
Erevu	Clever, talented	Kenya/ Tanzania

Names	Meanings	Origin
Ezeh	King, royalty	Nigeria
Ezima	Goodness	Nigeria
Fadhili	Kindness, goodwill	Kenya/ Tanzania
Fahari	Splendour	Kenya/ Tanzania
Fana	Spirited joy	Ethiopia
Fanaka	Prosperity	Kenya/ Tanzania
Fanikia	Prosperity	Kenya/ Tanzania
Faraja	Relief	Kenya/ Tanzania
Farisi	Competent, capable	Kenya/ Tanzania
Femi	Love me	Nigeria
Folorunhso	Under the care of God	Nigeria
Fumilayo	Give me joy	Nigeria
Gamal	Handsome	Egypt
Gantu	Giant	Uganda
Ghanima	Good fortune	Kenya/ Tanzania
Ghenet	Paradise	Ethiopia
Ghofiri	Forgiveness, pardon	Kenya/ Tanzania
Gilo	Let this live	Sierra Leone
Gobisa	Humble	South Africa
Gulu	Heaven	Uganda
Guntu	Giant	Uganda
Habibu	Beloved	Kenya/ Tanzania
Hadhi	Respect, honor	Kenya/ Tanzania
Haiba	Charm	Kenya/ Tanzania
Haile	Powerful	Ethiopia
Hakika	Truth	Kenya/ Tanzania
Halalisa	Compliment, praise	South Africa
Halili	Beloved one	Kenya/ Tanzania
Halisi	Truth	Kenya/ Tanzania
Hamadi	Tenacity	Kenya/ Tanzania
Hambisa	Progress	South Africa
Hashiki	Passion	Kenya/ Tanzania

Names	Meanings	Origin
Hatari	Harmless	Kenya/ Tanzania
Hazina	Treasure	Kenya/ Tanzania
Hekima	Clever, wise	Kenya/ Tanzania
Heshima	Highly esteemed	Kenya/ Tanzania
Heshimu	Honor, respect	Kenya/ Tanzania
Hiari	Free-will	Kenya/ Tanzania
Hidaya	Precious gift	Kenya/ Tanzania
Himidi	Praise be to God	Kenya/ Tanzania
Hindowah	Tough man	Sierra Leone
Hisani	Kind, good-natured	Kenya/ Tanzania
Hissa	Forgiveness, pardon	Kenya/ Tanzania
Hodari	Energetic, capable	Kenya/ Tanzania
Huba	Love, friendship	Kenya/ Tanzania
Huri	Free person	Kenya/ Tanzania
Huruma	Compassion, mercy	Kenya/ Tanzania
Hususa	Special	Kenya/ Tanzania
Ibada	Adoration	Kenya/ Tanzania
Ibibo	A nice and honest person	Nigeria
Ibiene	A beautiful day	Nigeria
Ibironke	Born into love	Nigeria
Ibroma	Be my guide	Nigeria
Idihi	Enthusiasm, perseverance	Kenya/ Tanzania
Idinga	Promise, vow	South Africa
Idiong	Prophet, one with foresight	Nigeria
Ifeanyi	Our beloved possession	Nigeria
Ifechi	God's very own	Nigeria
Ifeoma	A good thing	Nigeria
Ihejirika	Advantage	Nigeria
Ijeoma	Successful achievement	Nigeria
Ike	Power, authority	Nigeria
Ikechi	Power/might of God	Nigeria

Names	Meanings	Origin
Ikechuku	Power/might of God	Nigeria
Ikemba	People's power	Nigeria
Ikemefuna	My strength is for ever	Nigeria
Ikenna	God's/father's authority	Nigeria
Imamu	Minister, preacher	Kenya/ Tanzania
Imani	Faith, belief, religion	Kenya/ Tanzania
Imara	Stamina, strength	Kenya/ Tanzania
Imarika	Be steadfast	Kenya/ Tanzania
Ineada	Granny's favorite child	Nigeria
Ingelosi	Angel	South Africa
Inkonzo	Allegiance, loyalty	South Africa
Inkosi (Nkosi)	King, chief, Lord	South Africa
Inshallah	God willing	Kenya/ Tanzania
Insimi	Cheerfulness, merriment	South Africa
Isibili	Reality, truth	South Africa
Isibindi	Courageous, fearless	South Africa
Isifiso	Good wishes	South Africa
Isigebenga	Giant	South Africa
Isilahi	Reconciliation	Kenya/ Tanzania
Isilongo	Temptation	South Africa
Isiminya	Truth, reality	South Africa
Isimo	Quality	Kenya/ Tanzania
Isineke	Patience	Zimbabwe
Isintu	Mankind, humanity	South Africa
Isisa	Love, hospitality	South Africa
Isisila	Good luck	South Africa
Isithangami	Peace	South Africa
Isiyoshindika	Unconquerable	Kenya/ Tanzania
Isoka	Courageous, fearless	South Africa
Ituri	Sweet-smelling	Kenya/ Tanzania
Jabari	Almighty, omnipotent	Kenya/ Tanzania
Jahina	Brave, courageous	Kenya/ Tanzania

Names	Meanings	Origin
Jalali	Almighty/omnipotent	Kenya/ Tanzania
Jali	Respect, honor	Kenya/ Tanzania
Jamadari	Warrior, leader	Kenya/ Tanzania
Jamala	Friendly, good manners	Kenya/ Tanzania
Jana	Healthy child	Kenya/ Tanzania
Janna	Paradise	Kenya/ Tanzania
Jasiri	Fearless	Kenya/ Tanzania
Jinaki	Self-confident, proud	Kenya/ Tanzania
Jioni	Evening	Kenya/ Tanzania
Jirani	Neighbour	Kenya/ Tanzania
Jitu	Giant	Kenya/ Tanzania
Johari	Something valuable	Kenya/ Tanzania
Jumbe	Chief, VIP	Kenya/ Tanzania
Jumoke	Beauty is desirable	Nigeria
Jumu	Fate, luck	Kenya/ Tanzania
Juta	Regret	Kenya/ Tanzania
Kabaila	Person of high social status	Kenya/ Tanzania
Kabisa	For good	Kenya/ Tanzania
Kabona	Priest	Kenya/ Tanzania
Kadhi	Judge, wise person	Kenya/ Tanzania
Kafara	Sacrifice	Kenya/ Tanzania
Kahini	Priest, holy person	Kenya/ Tanzania
Kalamka	Intelligent, well-informed	Kenya/ Tanzania
Kalimba	Musical	Malawi
Kanai	Self-satisfied, contentment	Kenya/ Tanzania
Kanaifu	A self-sufficient person	Kenya/ Tanzania
Kani	Strength, energy	Kenya/ Tanzania
Kanye	Absolute, special, unique	South Africa
Kanzi	Treasure/valuable	Kenya/ Tanzania
Karama	Honor, respect, esteem	Kenya/ Tanzania

Names	Meanings	Origin
Karamu	Precious gift	Kenya/ Tanzania
Karimu	Generous, philanthropic	Kenya/ Tanzania
Kariuki	Born again	Kenya/ Tanzania
Kasisi	Priest, minister	Kenya/ Tanzania
Kaufulu	Freedom	Malawi
Kawaida	Natural	Kenya/ Tanzania
Kayode	Bring forth happiness	Nigeria
Keinba	The beautiful one	Nigeria
Kelechi	Praise the Lord	Nigeria
Kiaga	Promise	Kenya/ Tanzania
Kibali	Favor	Kenya/ Tanzania
Kibibi	Princess	Kenya/ Tanzania
Kiburi	Promise	Kenya/ Tanzania
Kidhi	Satisfaction	Kenya/ Tanzania
Kifaa	Useful	Kenya/ Tanzania
Kijana	Youthful, young	Kenya/ Tanzania
Kijani	Warrior/fearless	Kenya/ Tanzania
Kike	Feminine	Kenya/ Tanzania
Kimacho	Alert	Kenya/ Tanzania
Kimya	Calm, quiet	Kenya/ Tanzania
Kinaya	Self-sufficient	Kenya/ Tanzania
Kinuka	A type of flower	Kenya/ Tanzania
Kinyemi	Pleasant/something good	Kenya/ Tanzania
Kioja	Miracle	Kenya/ Tanzania
Kiongozi	Leader	Kenya/ Tanzania
Kipendo	Love, affection, devotion	Kenya/ Tanzania
Kipusa	Young girl	Kenya/ Tanzania
Kirafiki	Friendly	Kenya/ Tanzania
Kirimu	Generous, kind	Kenya/ Tanzania
Kisa	Mercy	Uganda
Kisasa	New, modern	Kenya/ Tanzania
Kitambi	The proud one/proud	Kenya/ Tanzania

Names	Meanings	Origin
Kito	Precious jewel	Kenya/ Tanzania
Kitoto	Sweet little child	Kenya/ Tanzania
Kiume	Masculine and strong	Kenya/ Tanzania
Kizo	Abundant, plentiful	Kenya/ Tanzania
Komboa	Redeemed, redemption	Kenya/ Tanzania
Kristo	Christian	Kenya/ Tanzania
Kroma	Deep thought, reflection	Nigeria
Kudumu	Very persevering	Kenya/ Tanzania
Kuforiji	Death please have mercy	Nigeria
Kulula	Superior, high quality	Kenya/ Tanzania
Kumbaka	Person with excellent memory	Kenya/ Tanzania
Kumbufu	Person with excellent memory	Kenya/ Tanzania
Kunjufu	Cheerful and friendly	Kenya/ Tanzania
Kupenda	Love	Kenya/ Tanzania
Kutisha	Tough, formidable	Kenya/ Tanzania
Kuweza	Very capable	Kenya/ Tanzania
Kwagalana	Brotherly love	Kenya/ Tanzania
Kwasi	Wealthy, self-sufficient	Kenya/ Tanzania
Kweli	Honesty, truth	Kenya/ Tanzania
Kwini	Queen	Kenya/ Tanzania
Kyesi	Joy	Kenya/ Tanzania
Laini	Gentle, soft	Kenya/ Tanzania
Lamamika	Pray for mercy	Kenya/ Tanzania
Lanre	Greatness	Nigeria
Latifu	Gentle, kind	Kenya/ Tanzania
Lipenga	Musical	Malawi
Liwaza	Consolation	Kenya/ Tanzania
Lola	Greatness	Nigeria
Lolia	Shining star	Nigeria
Lolo	Prosperity	Nigeria

Names	Meanings	Origin
Lomo	Sunshine	Nigeria
Luimba	Song	Uganda
Lukata	War lord	South Africa
Luleka	Caution	South Africa
Lulu	Orator	Kenya/ Tanzania
Maarifa	Knowledge	Kenya/ Tanzania
Mahiri	Skillful, clever	Kenya/ Tanzania
Mahungbe	Protector	Sierra Leone
Maimba	Song	Malawi
Maisha	Life	Kenya/ Tanzania
Majaliwa	By God's grace	Kenya/ Tanzania
Makini	Good character, exemplary leader	Kenya/ Tanzania
Malaika	Angel	Kenya/ Tanzania
Malenga	Good singer	Kenya/ Tanzania
Malkia	Queen	Kenya/ Tanzania
Maluum	Something special	Kenya/ Tanzania
Manani	Almighty	Kenya/ Tanzania
Manzili	Sent by God	Kenya/ Tanzania
Mapenzi	Pleasure	Kenya/ Tanzania
Marashi	Sweet air, pleasant	Kenya/ Tanzania
Marini	Attractive, very charming	Kenya/ Tanzania
Masamaha	Forgiveness	Kenya/ Tanzania
Mashuhuri	Fame	Kenya/ Tanzania
Masilahi	Reconciliation	Kenya/ Tanzania
Masiya	Messiah, Saviour	Kenya/ Tanzania
Matuko	Elegance	Kenya/ Tanzania
Mbingu	Heaven	Kenya/ Tanzania
Mbishiri	Prophet	Kenya/ Tanzania
Mcheshi	Very friendly	Kenya/ Tanzania
Mchumba	Sweetheart	Kenya/ Tanzania
Milele	Eternity	Kenya/ Tanzania

Names	Meanings	Origin
Mjibu	A nice person	Kenya/ Tanzania
Mjima	A helpful person	Kenya/ Tanzania
Mkristo	A Christian	Kenya/ Tanzania
Mkufunzi	Leader	Kenya/ Tanzania
Mkwasi	A wealthy person	Kenya/ Tanzania
Modupe	Thank God	Nigeria
Monima	Do not envy others	Kenya/ Tanzania
Moyo	Life	Malawi
Mpenzi	Lover, sweetheart	Kenya/ Tanzania
Mpingo	Ebony	Kenya/ Tanzania
Msaada	Help	Kenya/ Tanzania
Msanaa	A skillful man	Kenya/ Tanzania
Msemaji	Orator	Kenya/ Tanzania
Mshindi	Warrior	Kenya/ Tanzania
Mtaalamu	Intellectual and scholarly	Kenya/ Tanzania
Mtafiti	Knowledge seeker	Kenya/ Tanzania
Mtangulizi	Leader, pioneer	Kenya/ Tanzania
Mtawa	Religious/devout person	Kenya/ Tanzania
Mteremeshi	Genial and friendly	Kenya/ Tanzania
Mteremo	Cheerful person	Kenya/ Tanzania
Mteule	The chosen one	Kenya/ Tanzania
Mtoto	Youngster, little boy	Kenya/ Tanzania
Mtulivu	Quiet person	Kenya/ Tanzania
Mtume	An apostle	Kenya/ Tanzania
Mufari	Cheerfulness	Zimbabwe
Munda	Ours	Sierra Leone
Mungu	Fate, destiny	Kenya/ Tanzania
Munyenye	Star	Uganda
Muyaya	Forever	Malawi
Mzee	Elderly and wise, a sage	Kenya/ Tanzania
Mzuri	I feel good	Kenya/Nigeria

Names	Meanings	Origin
Nadhari	Personal choice, final decision	Kenya/ Tanzania
Nadhiri	Promise, vow	Kenya/ Tanzania
Nafaika	Prosperity	Kenya/ Tanzania
Nafasi	To love good times	Kenya/ Tanzania
Nafisi	To rescue	Kenya/ Tanzania
Nafisika	One who is well-off	Kenya/ Tanzania
Nakawa	Good-looking	Kenya/ Tanzania
Nawiri	Healthy-looking	Kenya/ Tanzania
Ndubisi	Life is precious	Nigeria
Nduka	Life is valuable	Nigeria
Neema	Graceful	Kenya/ Tanzania
Neemaka	Generous, benevolent	Kenya/ Tanzania
Negama	Famous, prominent	South Africa
Nemsi	Of good reputation, respectable	Kenya/Nigeria
Nenani	Explanation	Malawi
Nene	My beloved one	Nigeria
Nengi	Plentiful, abundant	Zimbabwe
Nepo	Comforter	Sierra Leone
Neratshi	Proud, self-assured	South Africa
Nesibindi	Courageous, fearless	South Africa
Nesisa	Generous, benevolent	South Africa
Nganga	Self-pride	Nigeria
Ngeri	Special, unique	Nigeria
Ngo	Wealth	Nigeria
Ngozi	Blessing	Nigeria
Nikela	Sacrifice	Zimbabwe
Nimi	Wisdom	Nigeria
Ningi	Abundant, plentiful	South Africa
Nishati	Full of vigor	Kenya/ Tanzania
Njema	Good	Kenya/ Tanzania

Names	Meanings	Origin
Njinga	Queen	South Africa
Nkechi	God's very own, chosen by God	Nigeria
Nkechika	God's own is the best	Nigeria
Nkem	My precious possession	Nigeria
Nkosi (Inkosi)	King, chief, Lord	South Africa
Nnameka	Praise/glory to God	Nigeria
Nteremezi	Friendly/cheerful person	Kenya/ Tanzania
Nufaika	Prosperity	Kenya/ Tanzania
Nurisha	Show the light	Kenya/ Tanzania
Nusurika	Saved from difficulty	Kenya/ Tanzania
Nweze	Royal child	Nigeria
Nyakeh	Just like father	Sierra Leone
Nyanda	Mine	Sierra Leone
Nyanga	Divine	South Africa
Nyemya	Respect, self-esteem	Kenya/ Tanzania
Nyikira	Perseverance	Uganda
Nyimba	Song	Uganda
Nyofu	Candid	Kenya/ Tanzania
Oba	King/nobility	Nigeria
Obi	Chief	Nigeria
Obioma	Clean mind	Nigeria
Obiora	The will of the people	Nigeria
Odusina	Hard work opens ways	Nigeria
Ofoma	Good-natured	Nigeria
Ogechi	God's time is the best	Nigeria
Ojike	Full of energy	Nigeria
Okechuku	Gift of God	Nigeria
Okorobia	Tough guy	Nigeria
Ola	Greatness, noble man	Nigeria
Olabisi	Greatness delivers	Nigeria
Olaniyi	This is greatness	Nigeria

Names	Meanings	Origin
Olatayo	Greatness deserves happiness	Nigeria
Olayinka	Greatness surrounds me	Nigeria
Olee	Happy moment	Nigeria
Oloye	One who earned the title	Nigeria
Olubayo	Great joy	Nigeria
Olufemi	God wants me	Nigeria
Olumeko	God	Nigeria
Olumide	My God is here	Nigeria
Olusegun	God conquers	Nigeria
Omari	Power/influential	Kenya/ Tanzania
Omasiri	Pleasant, very pleasing	Nigeria
Omotayo	A child is worth everything	Nigeria
Omuntu	An energetic person	Uganda
Omutonzi	The Creator, Almighty	Uganda
Ononye	Stay with me	Nigeria
Onyebuchi	God is greater than any human	Nigeria
Onyechi	Humans cannot play God	Nigeria
Onyekan	My turn to be king	Nigeria
Onyemachi	Nobody can figure out God	Nigeria
Onyemaechi	Nobody knows the future	Nigeria
Opara	My first male child	Nigeria
Opunabo	One with charisma	Nigeria
Pakribo	This is my answer/ response	Nigeria
Patanisha	Reconciliation	Kenya/ Tanzania
Penda	Lover, sweetheart	Kenya/ Tanzania
Pendo	Love	Kenya/ Tanzania

Names	Meanings	Origin
Penzima	Desire	Kenya/ Tanzania
Philisa	Remedy, answer	South Africa
Pulika	Obedience, obey	Kenya/ Tanzania
Radhi	Forgiveness	Kenya/ Tanzania
Rafiki	Trusted friend	Kenya/ Tanzania
Rahimu	Mercy	Kenya/ Tanzania
Rehani	Promise, vow	Kenya/ Tanzania
Rehema	Mercy	Kenya/ Tanzania
Remba	Beautiful	Kenya/ Tanzania
Ridhaa	Goodwill	Kenya/ Tanzania
Ridhisha	Satisfaction	Kenya/ Tanzania
Rotimi	My turn to be king	Nigeria
Saburi	Patience	Kenya/ Tanzania
Sadaka	Offering, sacrifice	Kenya/ Tanzania
Sadiki	Reliable friend	Kenya/ Tanzania
Sadikifu	Reliable friend	Kenya/ Tanzania
Sadikika	Trustworthy	Kenya/ Tanzania
Safi	Pure	Kenya/ Tanzania
Safidi	Clean, neat	Kenya/ Tanzania
Safisha	Cleansed, clean	Kenya/ Tanzania
Sala	Prayer	Kenya/ Tanzania
Salaam	Peace, tranquility	Kenya/ Tanzania
Salama	Peace, tranquility	Kenya/ Tanzania
Salamu	Perfect	Kenya/ Tanzania
Segun	Go and conquer	Nigeria
Selema	Be nice and fair to all	Nigeria
Shangilia	Happy occasion	Kenya/ Tanzania
Sharifu	Honorable, noble	Kenya/ Tanzania
Shasha	Champion	Zimbabwe
Shashu	Great joy	Ethiopia
Sheshe	Beauty, elegance	Kenya/ Tanzania
Sheyi	See what God did for me	Nigeria

Names	Meanings	Origin
Shiba	Beautiful lady	Ethiopia
Shibe	Satisfaction	Kenya/ Tanzania
Shibisha	Very satisfied	Kenya/ Tanzania
Shinda	Conqueror, victor	Kenya/ Tanzania
Shingayi	Perseverance	South Africa
Shirika	Trusted partner	Kenya/ Tanzania
Shukrani	Grateful	Kenya/ Tanzania
Sifa	Fame	Kenya/ Tanzania
Sikia	Harmony	Kenya/ Tanzania
Silika	Instinct	Kenya/ Tanzania
Simba	Tiger	Kenya/ Tanzania
Siri	Tiger	Nigeria
Siri	Secret	Kenya/ Tanzania
Soamakiri	Paradise, heaven	Nigeria
Sokipriye	Gift from God	Nigeria
Somieye	God's wish	Nigeria
Soyemi	Do I deserve this	Nigeria
Subira	Patience	Kenya/ Tanzania
Suluhu	Peacemaker	Kenya/ Tanzania
Tafiti	Knowledge seeker	Kenya/ Tanzania
Tajamali	Favor	Kenya/ Tanzania
Taji	Crown	Kenya/ Tanzania
Tajiri	Rich, wealthy	Kenya/ Tanzania
Takata	Pure, clean	Kenya/ Tanzania
Takatifu	Sacred, holy, saintly	Kenya/ Tanzania
Tamani	Praise	Malawi
Tamasha	Happy occasion	Kenya/ Tanzania
Tambika	Offering, sacrifice	Kenya/ Tanzania
Tambuzi	Intelligent, informed	Kenya/ Tanzania
Tamu	Sweet, pleasant, nice	Kenya/ Tanzania
Tamunosaki	God's time is the best	Nigeria
Tanashati	Well-dressed, neat	Kenya/ Tanzania

Names	Meanings	Origin
Taraji	Hope, faith	Kenya, Tanzania
Tarajika	Hope, faith	Kenya, Tanzania
Tarishi	Messenger	Kenya/ Tanzania
Tawa	A religious person	Kenya/ Tanzania
Tayari	Always ready	Kenya/ Tanzania
Teke	Prayer	Nigeria
Temba	Gift	South Africa
Temishe	Mine is done	Nigeria
Tendaji	Energetic	Kenya/ Tanzania
Terema	Friendly/cheerful person	Kenya/ Tanzania
Teremesha	Always willing to serve others	Kenya/ Tanzania
Thanda	Love	South Africa
Thibiti	Having a strong personality	Kenya/ Tanzania
Tiifu	Loyal, faithful	Kenya/ Tanzania
Tione	Let us see	Malawi
Tisha	Strong-willed	Kenya/ Tanzania
Tombi	Lovely	South Africa
Tonte	Destiny, providence	Nigeria
Tosha	Satisfaction	Kenya/ Tanzania
Tukufu	Dignified, respected, famous	Kenya/ Tanzania
Tulani	Peaceful	South Africa
Tulivu	Tranquility	Kenya/ Tanzania
Ubora	Excellence	Kenya/ Tanzania
Ubunengi	Abundance, plentiful	Zimbabwe
Ubuninzi	Abundance, plentiful	South Africa
Ubuntu	Humanity, mankind	Zimbabwe
Uche	Deep thought, reflection	Nigeria
Udoh	Second child	Nigeria
Uduak	Desire	Nigeria

Names	Meanings	Origin
Ufanisi	Prosperity	Kenya/ Tanzania
Ufefe	Grace	South Africa
Uheri	Good fortune	Kenya/ Tanzania
Uhuru	Freedom	Kenya/ Tanzania
Ujamaa	Family	Kenya/ Tanzania
Ukarimu	Hospitality	Kenya/ Tanzania
Ukulunga	Righteous	Zimbabwe
Ukurugenzi	Leader	Kenya/ Tanzania
Ukuthula	Peace	South Africa
Ukwazi	Knowledge	Zimbabwe
Umina	Ego	South Africa
Umuntu	Aristocrat; intellectual; saint	South Africa
Uncedo	Advantage	South Africa
Urafiki	Friendship	Kenya/ Tanzania
Ushindi	Victory	Kenya/ Tanzania
Usinga	Deep feelings	South Africa
Uwandi	Plentiful, abundant	Zimbabwe
Uzima	Energetic, vitality	Kenya/ Tanzania
Uzuko	Glory	South Africa
Uzuri	Beauty	Kenya/ Tanzania
Vamile	Abundant, plentiful	South Africa
Wadinasi	Freeman	Kenya/ Tanzania
Wakili	Hope, confidence	Kenya/ Tanzania
Wema	Virtue, kindness	Kenya/ Tanzania
Wenike	Power counts	Nigeria
Wepesi	Happiness	Kenya/ Tanzania
Weyni	Sweet/desire	?
Winbo	Song	Kenya/ Tanzania
Wingu	Heaven	Kenya/ Tanzania
Yakini	Truth/trust	Kenya/ Tanzania

Names	Meanings	Origin
Yeawa	This belongs to Grandma	Sierra Leone
Yingi	My beloved mother	Nigeria
Yomi	Save me	Nigeria
Zalimba	It is difficult	Malawi
Zena	Good news	Ethiopia
Zuri	Beautiful, georgeous	Kenya/ Tanzania

Appendices

Appendix A

African Language Groups and Subgroups

Niger-Kordofani Group:

a. Bantu (Kikuyu, Shona, Zulu, Xhosa, and Swahili)
b. Kwa (Yoruba, Ibo)
c. Mande (Malinke)
d. Fulani (Fula, Peul, Fulfulde)
e. Voltaic

Afro-Asiatic Group:

a. Ancient Egyptian
b. Berber
c. Amharic (Semitic)
d. Arabic
e. Somali
f. Chadic (Hausa)
h. Kushitic

Nilo-Saharan Group:

a. Songhai
b. Sudanic
c. Luo (Maasai)
d. Nubian
e. Mangbetu

Khoisan Group:

a. Hottentot
b. Sandawe
c. Hatsa (Kindiga, Hadza, Hadzapi)

Appendix B

Major African Language Groups

Appendix C

Language Subgroups and Regions of Dominance

Region	Dominant Language
East, Central, and South Africa	Swahili, Zulu, Xhosa,Kikuyu, and Shona.
West Africa	Ibo, Yoruba, Hausa, Fulani, Malinke, and Twi-Fante.
Sahara Region	Amharic (Semitic), Arabic, Berber, Somali, Kushitic, Nubian, and Songhai.
North African Region	Arabic, Berber, and Ancient Egyptian.

Appendix D

Early Kingdoms and Empires of Africa

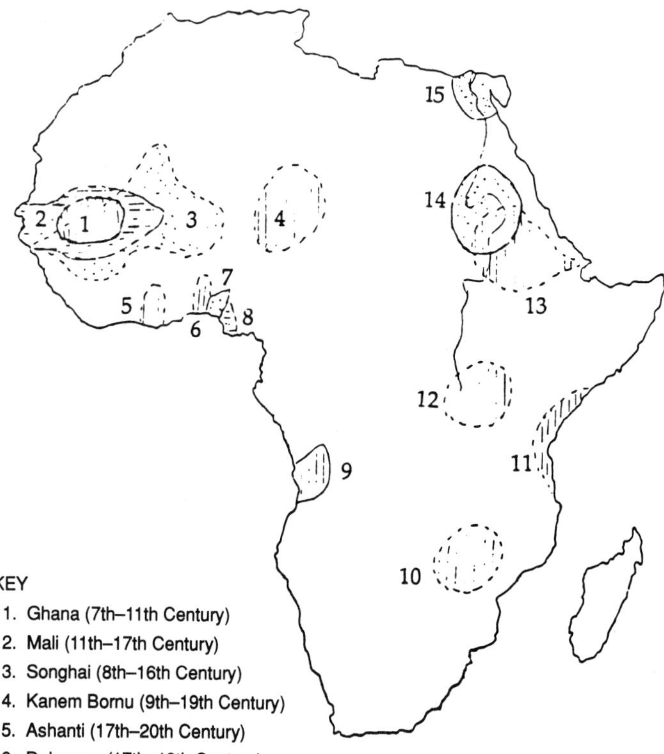

KEY

1. Ghana (7th–11th Century)
2. Mali (11th–17th Century)
3. Songhai (8th–16th Century)
4. Kanem Bornu (9th–19th Century)
5. Ashanti (17th–20th Century)
6. Dahomey (17th–19th Century)
7. Oyo (13th–19th Century)
8. Benin (12th–19th Century)
9. Kongo (15th–18th Century)
10. Mwene-Mutapa (Zimbabwe) (16th–17th Century)
11. Zenj City-States (11th–16th Century)
12. Lake Kingdoms (13th–20th Century)
13. Aksum (1st–8th Century)
14. Kush (10th Century B.C.–3rd Century A.D.)
15. Ancient Egypt (5000 B.C.–7th Century)

Appendix E

Countries of Africa

Bibliography

Adams, William. *Nubia: Corridor to Africa.* Princeton: Princeton University Press, 1977.

Anderson, S.E. "Mathematics and the Struggle for Black Liberation." *The Black Scholar* (September, 1970).

Alfred, C. *Art in Ancient Egypt.* London: Alec Tiranti, 1969.

Aptheker, Herbert. *A Documentary History of the Negro People in the United States from Colonial Times Through the Civil War.* New York: Citadel Press, 1967.

Bastide, Roger. *African Civilization in the New World.* New York: Harper Torch Books, 1971.

Battuta, Ibn. *Travels in Asia and Africa 1325–1354.* New York: Augustus M. Kelley, 1969.

Bell, Derik J. *Race, Racism and American Law.* Boston: Little, Brown and Company, 1973.

Benedict, Ruth. *Race: Science and Politics.* New York: Viking, 1959.

Ben-Jochanan, Yosef. *African Origin of the Major "Western Religions."* New York: Alkebu-Lan Books, 1970.

———. *Africa, Mother of Western Civilization.* New York: Alkebu-Lan Books, 1971.

———. *Cultural Genocide in the Black and African Studies Curriculum.* New York: Alkebu-Lan Books, 1972.

———. *A Chronology of the Bible: Challenge to the Standard Version.* New York: Alkebu-Lan Books, 1973

———. *The Black Man's Religion: The Myth of Genesis and*

Exodus and the Exclusion of Their African Origin. New York: Alkebu-Lan Books, 1974.

Blyden, J. W. *Christianity, Islam, and Negro Race*. Edinburgh: Edinburgh University Press, 1967: 1887.

Bontemps, Arna. *Great Slave Narratives*. Boston: Beacon Press, 1969.

Brent, Peter. *Black Nile: Mungo Park and the Search for the Niger*. New York: Gordon Cremonesi, 1977.

Burgmann, Peter M. and Mort N. Burgmann. *The Chronological History of the Negro in America*. New York: Mentor Books, 1969.

Chineweizu, O. *The West and the Rest of Us: White Predators, Black Slaves and African Elite*. New York: Vintage Books, 1975.

Churchward, Albert. *The Signs and Symbols of Primordial Man: The Evolution of Religious Doctrines from the Eschatology of the Ancient Egyptians*. Westport: Greenwood Press, 1978: 1913.

Clegg, Legrand H. "The Beginning of the African Diaspora: Black Men in Ancient Medieval America." Los Angeles, 1977.

Collins, Robert O. *Problems in African History*. Englewood Cliffs, N.J.: Prentice Hall, 1968.

Cooley, W. D. *The Negroland of the Arabs Examined and Explained: An Inquiry into the Early History and Geography of Central Africa*. Frank Cass and Co. Ltd., 1966.

Cox, George O. *African Empires and Civilizations*. Washington, D.C.: African Heritage Publishers, 1974.

Cruse, Harold. *The Crises of the Negro Intellectual*. New York: William Morrow, 1967.

Davidson, Basil. *Old Africa Rediscovered*. London: Victor Gollanez Ltd., 1970.

———. *African Kingdoms.* New York: Time-Life Books Inc., 1971.

———. *Discovering Our African Heritage.* Boston: Gina and Co., 1971.

Diop, Cheikh Anta. *The African Origin of Civilization: Myth or Reality.* New York: Lawrence Hill and Col., 1974: 1955.

Dobthofer, Ernest. *Voices in Stone: The Decipherment of Ancient Scripts and Writings.* New York: Collier, 1971.

Erny, Pierre. *Childhood and Cosmos: The Social Psychology of the Black African Child.* New York: Black Orpheus Press, 1973: 1968.

Evans, Judith L. *Children in Africa: A Review of Psychological Research.* New York: Teacher's College Press, 1970.

Fage, J. D. and R. A. Oliver. *Papers in African Prehistory.* Cambridge: Harvard University Press, 1970.

Fanon, Frantz. *Black Skin White Masks.* New York: Grove, 1967.

Fell, Barry. *America B.C.: Ancient Settlers in the New World.* New York: Wallaby, 1976.

Fon, Horsemann. *Black American Scholars: A Study of Their Beginnings.* Detroit, Mich.: Balamp Publishers, 1971.

Freyre, Gilberto. *The Masters and the Slaves.* New York: Alfred A. Knopf, Inc., 1946.

Graves, Kersey. *The World's Sixteen Crucified Saviours: Christianity Before Christ.* New York: Truth Seekers Press, 1975: 1875.

Gregory, Dick. *No More Lies: The Myth and Reality of American History.* New York: Harper and Row, 1971.

Gross, Seymour L., and J. E. Hardy (eds.) *Images of the Negro in American Literature.* Chicago: The University of Chicago Press, 1966.

Harris, Joseph E. (ed.). *Africa and Africans As Seen by Classical Writers: The William Leo Hansberry African History*

Notebook, Volume II. Washington, D.C.: Howard University Press, 1977.

Harris, Joseph E. *Africans and Their History.* New York: Mentor, 1972.

Herskovitis, Melville J. *The Myth of the Negro Past.* Boston: Beacon Press, 1969.

Hodge, J. L., D. K. Struckmann and Lynn D. Trost. *Cultural Basis of Racism and Group Oppression: An Examination of Traditional Western Concepts, Values and Institutional Structures Which Support Racism, Sexism and Elitism.* Berkeley: Two Riders Press, 1975.

Idowu, E. Bolaji. *African Traditional Religion: A Definition.* New York: Orbis Books, 1975.

Ions, Veronica. *Egypt Mythology.* London: Hamlyn, 1965.

Jackson, John G. *Introduction to African Civilizations.* Secaucus, New Jersey: The Citadel Press, 1974: 1970.

Jahn, Janheinze. *Muntu: The New African Culture.* New York: Grove, 1961.

James, George G. M. *Stolen Legacy.* San Francisco, Ca.: Julian Richardson, 1976. (First published 1954.)

Jay, James M. *Negroes in Science: Natural Science Doctorates, 1876–1969.* Detroit, Mich.: Balamp Publishers, 1971.

Johnson, J. C. deGraft. *African Glory: The Story of Vanished Negro Civilizations.* New York: Walker, 1954.

Johnson, Samuel. *The History of the Yorubas from Earliest Times to the Beginning of the British Protectorate.* Lagos, Nigeria. CSS Bookstore (P.O. Box 174, 50 Broad Street, Lagos, Nigeria), 1976: 1921.

King, Keneth. *Pan Africanism and Education: A Study of Race, Philanthropy and Education in the Southern States of America and East Africa.* Oxford: Clarendon Press, 1971.

Lesbau, Wolf. *Falasha Anthology: The Black Jews of Ethiopia* (Translated from Ethiopian Sources). New York: Schocken, 1951.

Mannix, D. P. and M. Crowley. *Black Cargoes: A History of the Atlantic Slave Trade 1518–1865.* New York: Viking, 1962.

Mbiti, John S. *African Religions and Philosophy.* New York: Praeger, 1979.

Massey, Gerald. *Ancient Egypt, the Light of the World: A Work of Reclamation and Restitution in Twelve Books.* New York: Samuel Weiser, Inc., 1973: 1907.

Mitchell, Henry H. *Black Belief: Folk Belief in Blacks in America and West Africa.* New York: Harper and Row Publishers, 1975.

Montagu, Ashley (ed.). *The Concept of the Race.* London: Collier, 1964.

Morel, E.D. *The Black Man's Burden: The White Man in Africa from the Fifteenth Century to World War 1.* New York: Modern Reader Paperbacks, 1969.

Murphy, Jefferson E. *History of African Civilization.* New York: Dell, 1972.

Noble, Jeanne. *Beautiful Also Are the Souls of My Black Sisters: A History of the Black Woman in America.* Englewood Cliffs, N.J.: Prentice Hall, 1978.

Obadele, I. and A. Obadele. *Civilization Before the Time of Christ.* Detroit: The History of Songhay, 1975.

Oliver, R. and C. Oliver (eds.). *Africa in the Days of Exploration.* Englewood Cliffs, N.J.: Prentice Hall, 1965.

Osei, G. K. *African Contribution to Civilization.* London: The African Publication Society, 1973.

Price, R. (ed.). *Maroon Societies: Rebel Slave Communities in the Americas.* New York: Doubleday, 1973.

Rice, L. D. *The Negro in Texas 1874–1900.* Baton Rouge: Louisiana State University Press, 1971.

Rodney, Walter. *How Europe Underdeveloped Africa.* Washington: Howard University Press, 1974.

Rogers, Joel A. *Nature Knows No Color Line: Research into the*

Negro Ancestry in the White Race. New York: Helga M. Rogers, 1952.
———. *Africa's Gift to America*. New York: Helga M. Rogers, 1956.
———. *The World's Great Men of Color*. New York: Collier Macmillan, 1972.
Rout, Leslie B. *The African Experience in Spanish America 1502 to the Present Day*. New York: Cambridge University Press, 1976.
Sidren, Ben. *Black Talk*. New York: Holt, Rhinehart and Winston, 1971.
Snowden, Frank M., Jr. *Blacks in Antiquity: Ethiopians in the Greco-Roman Experience*. Cambridge: Harvard University Press, 1971.
Van Sertma, Ivan. *They Came before Columbus*. New York: Random House, 1976.
Walker, David. *Walker's Appeal: An Address to the Slaves of the United States of America*. New York: Arnold Press, 1969: 1829.
Walsh, M. *The Ancient Black Christians*. San Francisco: Julian Richardson, 1969.
Weathermax, John M. *The African Contribution: Parts I and II*. Los Angeles: The John Henry and May Louisa Dun Bryant Foundation, 1968.
Whitten, N. E., Jr. *Black Frontiermen: A South American Case*. New York: Schenkman, 1974.
Wiener, Leo. *Africa and the Discovery of America*. New York: Kraus Reprint Company, 1971: 1920.
William, Chancellor. *The Destruction of Black Civilization: Great Issues of a Race 4500 B.C. to 2000 A.D.* Chicago: Third World Press, 1974.
Williams, Robert L. (ed.). *Ebonics: The True Language of Black Folks*. St. Louis: Institute of Black Studies.
Windsor, R. R. *From Babylon to Timbuktu; A History of Ancient*

Black Races Including the Black Hebrews. New York: Oxford University Press, 1966.

Woodson, Carter G. *Miseducation of the Negro.* Washington, D.C.: The Associated Publishers, Inc., 1969: 1933.

———. *African Heroes and Heroines.* Washington, D.C.: The Associated Publishers, Inc., 1969.

———. *The History of Negro Church.* Washington, D.C.: The Associated Publishers, Inc., 1972: 1921.

———. *The Negro in Our History.* Washington, D.C.: The Associated Publisher, Inc., 1972: 1922.

Woodward, C. Vann. *The Strange Career of Jim Crowe.* New York: Oxford University Press, 1966.

X, Malcolm. *On African-American History.* New York: Pathfinder Press, 1967.

To the Reader

This book is not a listing of all African names. More names will be included in the next edition. If you would like your name and its meaning to be considered for the next edition, please send both to: S. Opunabo Abell, c/o Vantage Press, 516 West 34th Street, New York, N.Y. 10001.